JAMES CONOR PATTERSON is from Newry in the north of
Ireland. He won an Eric Gregory Award for *bandit country* in
2019 and fragments and versions of these poems have appeared
in publications such as *Magma, The Moth, New Statesman, Poetry
Ireland Review, The Poetry Review, The Stinging Fly, Poetry London*
and *The Tangerine*. A selection of James' poems was shortlisted
for *The White Review Poet's Prize*. His journalism and non-fiction
have been published in *The Guardian, i-D* and *The Irish Times*
among others. He is editor of the anthology *The New Frontier:
Reflections from the Irish Border*. He currently lives in London.

James Conor Patterson

bandit country

PICADOR

First published 2022 by Picador
an imprint of Pan Macmillan
6 Briset Street, London EC1M 5NR
EU representative: Macmillan Publishers Ireland Ltd, 1st Floor,
The Liffey Trust Centre, 117–126 Sheriff Street Upper, Dublin 1 D01 YC43
Associated companies throughout the world
www.panmacmillan.com

ISBN 978-1-5290-9277-6

1 3 5 7 9 8 6 4 2

A CIP catalogue record for this book is available from the British Library.

Printed and bound by TJ Books Ltd, Padstow, Cornwall

for aimée walsh and my family
and in memory of maureen patterson (née parks)

if i could sleep standing, i would wait here
for ever, become a landmark, something fixed
for tug crews or seabound passengers to point at,
an example of being part of a place.

— douglas dunn, 'landscape with one figure'

Contents

bandit country

bambooland

as one put drunk intae the back of a parent's car—
seized, it'd seem, by the adolescent desire

to be remindeda one's failins—this mornin
saw me retorn t bambooland near john martin gardens.

i went alone—sporred as i had bin in previous years
by the cousin who supplied the sprite-bottle lung, the beer,

the suitea cobbled forniture pilfered outta skips . . .
back then wid sit fer hours atop broken doors & pallets

until one of us—suddenly compelled t danger—
would gaze square intae the bamboo void an bid the other

jump! as though nahin at all'd stop us.
as though naither one had thought, like orpheus,

that t descend in order t retrieve might lave us
head propped against the lyre; might see us

ascend again wi scuffmarks wound beneath the skin
and trailed by the scents of bamboo oak & whin.

may queens

there we were at the barracks arch near linenhall square,
lukin—for all we were worth—like a cuppla vaudeville performers
in our ma's old barbara stanwyck shurtwaists & revlon red
   lipsticks;
me in my sister's pater pan-collar blouse an dance-it-up heels.

fabulous to a fault, we spent the afternoon collectin pennies
in a washed-out soup can, paradin our broom-handle maypole like
   a banner
and readyin our mates for placement on the canal's middle bank
where wid morris dance freely until we were called for tea.

there wid muddy our knees t set the thing straight—twistin this
   way
then the ohr—until we met at its base, an the eggshells plucked
from yesterday's rubbish cascaded down our hawthorn coronets
   like rain;
our folks entreatin t good-room virgins: *mercy, mercy fer their sins.*

yew

at which point the saint lifted
a fallen aril and placed it in his alb,
carryin it for miles until he reached

the head of a desolate valley strand,
whereupon—seein only growths
of sweetbrar in the mottled sand—

he removed the thing and placed it
in a small hole, invoking: *though
only the smallest of seeds, yet growing,*

*shall become the tallest of all things,
a tree.* durin which time the aril split
and a yew borst slowly intae life,

rufflin the sweetbrar & patrick's stole,
pointin its way t ward heaven & cryin,
my god, this is where i'm rooted.

currents

thinka two young rapscyallions launchin their newspaper boat—*as fragile as a may butterfly*—down a flagstone culvert with a rusted grille . . .

what wonders! t see spricks the relative sizea cattle hauled onboard yer unsteady vessel, an t jorney, tin soldier, intae a dark where the only sourcea natural light is the glare from a *starbucks* takeaway cup.

one dry tear punctuating 'bliss'

which is t say no tear atall, *prose fly*,
but a thought that threads the air
like craquelure through a michelangelo:
this chipped plasterboard, this bay window.

those forst few days in liverpool
my heart was a tangle of unhoovered dog hair,
and when i scrubbed the *IKEA* feldspar mugs
so hard they shone like ronde-bosse enamel,

i felt ye buzz intae my reflection a moment
and ask just what it was: this coffee-stained
elegies on the inside pocketa my coat;
this thing one feels fer home away from home

when, as dunn has it, i have *been inside*
my head . . . falling in love, preparing this good life.

about suffering

so many of us gathered that ye'd think
we were about t levitate the town hall;
freaks of ivry stripe—from navvies ankle-deep
in concrete dust, t pensioners, schoolteachers, councilmen,
    the ecumenical—
callin down the moutha the crimean war cannon
like oracles charmin apollo from the rocks . . .
am somewhere near the back, among that sun-bleached portion
of a stranger's bad polaroid—probly drunk,
probly pitchin
memorial arcs of strongbow down the arts centre steps—
when outta nowhere, a saracen comes squealin
through the barricades and our handiwork is scyattered all over
    kildare st:
bornt-out cars, wash pots, empty kegs, cinder blocks.

the sorta thing i imagine there mighta bin
had i lived through the eighties; as the unheard of, unseen
narrator of an altoger
grottier icarus—wearin my german army surplus coat
& battered derbys—who can't seem t articulate
the insidiousness of failure as sanctioned by the state.
i think about this, and about my parents & brors,
press *book selected flights* and i go back home t vote.

mug

spose it's midnight, and yer at the mouth
of a deserted, dimly-lit subway
on lower water st . . . spose ye shout/
sing the words *tiocfaidh ár lá* down the uvulae
of this piss-befouled, several-throated beast,
then hear the borsta glass on pebbledash.
spose the sourcesa this—in their nike trackies,
an wi scarves pulled tight intae riot masks—
appear next t ye like virgil, then speakin,
ask for yer phone or they'll *fuck you up* . . .
what would *you* do? spose they're tweakin,
for example, and this bein a holdup,
threaten ye with a knife then fracture yer nose . . .
spose this comes to define ye. spose.

sanctuary

midway through mi own fuckin *life's journey*—
since am twenty nai, an destined for such things
as premature death from stroke at forty—

i wake t find myself among the high ceilins
of st colman's cathedral on hill st;
perched, like a madman, next t some martins

with only a two-bar heater for heat.
i wake alone, with the choirmaster's podium
jammed agin the doora this choir loft suite,

carvin my name outta pure tedium
intae one of the pipes on the pipe organ,
when suddenly i hear chantin—as at a stadium—

erupt in the street, and father morgan
remonstratin from the church's front door
that *nai wid be the time* since am upstairs, snorin.

am flabbergasted! a thought a was bein ignored
by the aul bastard, and had sorta hoped—
that with the exceptiona the odd hoor

from st christopher's park & some dope—
i could live mi days in relative peace
under the watchful eye of john paul, our pope.

hadn't figured that, of all people, the priest
wid be the one t grass me t my captors,
who're on their way up nai t bag up ma knees.

the drowning

the story then became like this:
>he'd jumped in off a clydesdale horse,

then vanished like eurydice
>beneath the sawdust oil & gorse.

his friends went lukin for him there,
>sun scorched in their wool-knit pants,

beneath the rusted excavator
>up from high st & the manse.

they brought corned beef & bitsa soda,
>wrapped up ina greaseproof square,

they tuk some choclate from the soldiers,
>*d'arcy's* kept in earthenware,

and checked the crushers filled with ashlar,
>the morris tipper & the track,

decided they would jump in also
>when they failed t bring him back.

and so the parents brought their hammers,
>bitsa sheathin, casin nails,

and built a mast from railway sleepers,
>darnin suntans fer their sails,

and built a boat to cross the quarry,
>divin where their kids went in,

and fallaed them intae the hollow
>which locals said had no bottom.

and so the mayor dived for the parents,
>worried for his yearly vote,

and so the council braved the currents

                          for their leader's anecdote,

and then the dactors & the soldiers,

                          fallaed by the entire town,

until at last they filled the swimhole

                          and all of us wor underground.

wildcat

you return from the eco-friendly outhouse after dark with yer face a shade paler, even, than what the glow from this well-timed full moon might educe, or the looka disgust achieved ivry time you have t flush with two shovelsa sawdust ana helpin of bottled rainwater . . .

i know sometin's up, an am sorry i wasn't there t protect you from the cyat. the cyat, you say, who crouched like a ninja in the open doorway, and was ready either to lape at you an lave me destitute— without reason or a way back north—or t perch in yer lap as i've done, many times, needin some forma rescue from the wild it claims t inhabit.

so we might as well apologise for some other things, this cyat & i . . . like wat, for instance, are we doin in a tepee in the west of ireland, removed from all but ourselves & the moon? what is that noise we both make when we wanna get your attention, fallin somewhere within the known decibel range, but high pitched and in any case inaudible to anyone else but you?

yer not even awake to hear me whisper this: tryin t rationalise what happens in a remote forest as somehow symbolic of our bond; of me & you anol this cockamamie poetry i claim t enjoy so much; of this cyat who—by virtue of bein both wild & unknowable—is also immense, inevitable as a *sidhe*.

the spiritualists

thinkin thena the mcginn widow—
to whom a caul-wrapped stillborn was bestowed

by the passagea time & local rumour—
that wi word seen through a ripped strainer,

she'd have us cleaved in two
by the enda my english breakfast or yours . . .

that for the sake of an extra tenner,
she'd open themara like the cadaver

of her caul-wrapped boy, an end us
with a word; this bridget cleary, this *tasseomancer.*

i think again, love, that t believe in this
would be t chapen the accident of our own gift:

a shared impulse over gins at *the garrick,*
two photons kept unobserved through the double-slit.

*

greedy fer my own derangement, i pulled
a six-foot swatcha cheesecloth from my gullet

like a never-endin hanky—passed it
around the livin room proclaimin, *magic!*

then spokea how it was this resurrected *thing.*
next, i tugged on a hidden catgut string

so that the light disappeared, an in the fuss
that follaed, a man outlined in phosphorus

steered intae view & moved agin the gloom.
meanwhile, a reachin rod thrust about the room

and all around me was *chaos! chaos!*
i fuckin loved it when my house was in séance.

brotherswater

brother. when the storm came, the wind assailed my mouth.

it spoke its object and said *welcome brother*, so i said *welcome brother* back.

when it said *jackdaw*, the alders cantered their russet mountain, and the lake continued its onward expanse toward nowhere.

a sheep lay dead in a busted liner with its legs protruding like the broken pieces of a mop.

the farmer whose land it was seemed uninterested or not at home or both, and two half-shells of perfect coconut hung tied to a footbridge with ragged loops of twine.

none of these seemed bad omens.

were i to tell you that back in november i got fired from my job for chemically adjusting to sertraline—

that the sun was shining, unseasonably warm, into the centre of our flat, and it was so close to christmas that i could practically taste my dinner—

how could you tell me that *these* were not the extant auguries of collapse?

consider my position then & my position now as corresponding runes in a muddled forecast.

consider the storm, and the ways in which the lake has already foretold its name.

come on in, brother. the water is electric.

the disappeared

even now i find it difficult to imagine
being a campesino—dicing sweet potato
over the kitchen sink—my hands calloused
from years of raising sugarcane & lemon.
what could possibly be to such a life?
argentina is tending more important matters.
i hand out leaflets in the monteros for santucho.
in january a transport plane is shot down
and kills thirteen. i'm not sorry.
perón is not in power, so civility can rise again
in the green-cut mountains of tucamán
like christ removing lazarus's shroud.
the sun shimmering off la angostura.
the blue & white of the flag in cloudless sky.

and with these things when they come,
they wrap me like a present. sometime
close to dawn—with an oil rag in my mouth
and a bloodstained pillowcase wrapped
around my head—i'm thrown from a helicopter
into the south atlantic and sent to greet the fish.
the last thing i hear is *traitor* or its equivalent.
i have no frame of reference. the ocean
carries me over thousands of miles
and when i'm disturbed again, i'm something else
entirely: a rumour in the sand, perhaps, or a ghost
without pasture; someone who might be a shell
or a fossil, foundations on an unfinished house,
or four converged headlamps on a quiet country road.

bar story

that night he takes the freight ferry
from heysham t warrenpoint,
an stands by the railin of the upper car deck,
smokin embassy regals, and flickin pages
from an annotated a5 copybook intae the irish sea.
this is the acta givin back eucharist:
names, dates, newspaper clippins, sketches
of old girlfriends, addresses, phone numbers;
memorabilia useful t no one.
they leave his hands like frightened burds.
later, he'll meet my ma
in a sawdust dive on francis st,
after spendin hours with his own father & uncle,
standin drinks an leafin through
a beer-soaked copy of *an phoblacht*.
he tells me this in the café iruña
in pamplona—twenty five years later—
in front of a giant floor to ceilin length mirror
castin golden light back & forth
ontae our table like a private quasar.
am noddin an shakin my head
intermittently, listenin to my da's advice,
an tryin to imagine bein more
than just the unintended consequence
of two kids who took to marriage.
but it's difficult. between him & me,
things get summoned t inhabit our circle

like ouija, an as his story plays out,
someone does an accent, someone else a face,
and when the punchline finally arrives
we laugh, cause naither one of us is talkin.

[elegy]

after this, a sweepa dark tahoma spackles the VDU & a gr8
outpourin fills the page—as mass cards might—wen a wake
is closed & condolences pile beneath a crk in the front door.

yr head's cocked unnaturally t one side of the thumbnail.
yr still joy's caught between yr relationship status & the cover photo
of a lost weekend like colored glass in a saint's mausoleum.

i evn consider signin the guestbook wen it hpns. tributes stick
in the ether as canopic jars filled with organs & animal mummies,
an six months dwn the line, i'll poke bk & wonder if it's real.

prosopagnosia

frozen, on the top street in barcroft—
an lukin out over the town splayed
on the valley floor below
like a shattered bauble—
i await yer call then see the car.

our 2004 silver volvo sedan,
parked beneath a streetlight
on the ohr sidea the road,
with a man inside.
his hands around the steerin wheel
like hands around a crackin branch.
his face on the inner convex
of the tinted windshield, unshaven,
breathin our cherry-scented air
and worryin aloud
via speaker-phone over the low huma
the archers on radio four.
i worry about coins in the change tray
an jellies in the glove compartment,
an wonder if the odometer glowin
in his face might put him off
any notion he has of theft.

so i ask, gettin in, *how're things?*
t which he looks at me noddin,
back t bein you,
the seats frayed imitation leather
warmin beneath us both
as you carry me home in the dark—
trustin that someone wasn't plagiarisin
your creator's blueprints
for a doppelganger,
an that my own creator
remains beside me, drivin.

ghost estates

in eacha these i picture the dead
wrapped in carrion, as in evenin wear
for the gatherina some smart party.

their lips puckered an shrank,
renderin silence; their shoes warped
an legs buckled, though carried somehow

wi the gracea no longer bein—
of separation from the livin,
who buy houses they'll niver inhabit,

with money they'll niver accumulate,
on time which is speculative,
limited, an niver guaranteed.

the overmantle

by the time i'd introduced myself
to the space between the good room windows,
i was snuff-coloured, frangible as delft,

ungainly in giltwood & gesso,
though so taken with the mirror on the shelf
opposite, that when we first exchanged info,

i saw myself reflected in new light; felt
that with each regression i was shown,
that a younger, better me was being dealt.

*

a younger, better me when pride of place
was taken in the old man's living room.
when the georgian pediment's fuchsias

appeared, not so much carved, as in bloom,
and the glass which had just been replaced
took stills the quality of an optical-zoom

camera . . . for as long as i occupied this space
i was understood as more than just the heirloom,
being, all at once: twin, companion, nemesis.

*

now i'm relegated to bric-a-brac
relapsing infinitely into my opposite,
my opposite into me. we've gone back

almost as far as the miner's drawing out
silver ore & tin to make glass from rock,
when suddenly, out of a composite

of past selves, comes a door opening a crack
and a man observing himself through its slit.
he's saying, *bring me back, bring me back.*

xanadu

if they ask me was i happy
when he croaked it, i'd have to say no.
i wouldn't wish on anybody
a fate like that, let alone the dandy
      who'd kept me in his home.
i worked three laborious years,
flitting beneath that feature chandelier
like a trapped moth, argued with him about the placemats
when he finally opened up his pleasure dome
to guests, and was promptly given the sack
for telling him where they should go . . .

but enough about that. the man had a wife
& kids after all, and to speak ill of the dead
at this point feels like plunging his corpse with a knife.
feels like ransacking each compartment of his life,
finding a gun & shouting, *look at this instead!*
should it matter, for example, that for the cost
of some lacquered japanese commode, jobs were lost?
or that for each *pietra dura* tile
in his swimming pool's walls, lawsuits were filed?
perhaps . . . but why should it be my place
to bash the boss or talk about his estate?
consider that if i'd been born in the flophouse
to an unwed mother during blackout,
i too might've lost all perspective
about how much money was too much;

might've spent *my* life chasing some cartier watch
while all around me kindness was elective.
i'd have entombed myself within high-ceilinged rooms,
surrounded by georgian style candelabrums,
    talked to the hellenic replicas
    of venus de milo & ares,
    then read the glass-cased manuscript
    of *vetus latina* that i'd ripped
from the grasp of the national museum . . .
the better to keep in my mausoleum.

on meeting an influence at a book signing

abrasive. swishin moscato like a plug
of masticated chaw, he spat, *name?*
then eyed me like i was there t flog
his signature all over ebay. *james,*
i replied, before slinkin off in a fume.
so if yer readin this, *d*—unlikely
as ye are to—spend some time in a room
darkened by yer own bitter irony,
an reflect, that you're as nothin
when compared with mi own dead grandfather,
who fabricated steel for a livin
an knew that words like these held no water.
for fuck's sake! he'd say, weldin part of a gate.
why are ye here if ye can't hold it straight?

altnaveigh

what was the namea that aul neighbour's house?
the one who claimed to've welded pipes in the *harp*
factry in dundalk where he saw rats
simperin headlong over the tops
of mash tuns, yeast fermenters
& copper kettles built for sturrin beer mix.

i can't remember im ever drinkin the mix,
though ivry one'd whisper about the house
across from ours, complete with home-fermentation
kit, *james last* on vinyl, tricolour, harp,
copya the proclamation, a few scattered bottletaps,
and an overgrown garden filled wi rats.

distant relatives circled like rats
until the day he finally got so mixed up,
he wandered himself over the tap
of a car bonnet an got put inside a rest home.
there was no serenade, no harp,
no fiddle, an he was left to foment

in the same place we all someday go to foment.
his house was left as fodder for the rats.
his relatives could find no use for the harp,
the tricolour, the vinyl, or the useless mix
of other bric-a-brac that inhabited the house,
so they threw it all over the tap

of a hired skip—close to where he lies—waitin to be topped,
workin an iron lung instead of a yeast fermenter.
a plethora of norses at the home
keep im company in lieu of his rats
and evry evenin he's given a mixture
of pills. evry so often he asks for a tastea *harp,*

but when he does, his norse just laughs. *there's no harp*
here, she says. *an if there was i'd be top*
of the bloody queue! he laughs too, but his is a mix
of understandin an bein demented;
his mind havin been left t rot
where even his memories fail t take him home:

to the house next t mine with no harp,
rats in the garden, tricolour, bottletaps,
or smell of fermented home brew. to life's peculiar mix.

maturity date

it's not that am afraid, grandda,
of you or yer carpet-slippered
revenant hauntin the trevor hill
bank of ireland like a pulse from
the silent alarm; nor of my own
face caught again in plexiglas at
the cashier window, surrendered
to its guise of yours, though
weak jawed an crooked from an
afternoon spent consolidatin debt
options an bordered by financial
advice, but of bein here, years
from now, an ghostin my way
through the bank's mullioned
windaes like groundwater pulled
through the wand of a dowser,
because when i finally come face
t face with my own younger
image, assessin each personal
loan, negotiatin some long-term
repayment package, i'll have to
say to him then, as you say t me
nai, that this is the diffrence
between life & death.

on returning from the hospital, my granny

adjusted the horn of her hearin aid
so that the frequency shifted,
then screeched, then silence descended
through an open window—
as though burds had landed,
or flors settled in the sill.
fair city prattled on mute in the background.
a distant kettle popped in the larder,
an *what was it ye wanted to ask me*
bandied between us for sevral moments,
though i could thinka nahin—
an enquiry intae the new priest, perhaps,
or an anecdote about her da's time at ypres—
whereupon, settlin herself
intae the wingback seat that was mi grandda's,
she gave an account of wat it was like t fly.

ENGLAND

by sixteen he'd holed up in a smog-blackened terrace on the islea
dogs, plyin his trade as a labourer, an playin frames down the mile
end american pool & snooker club where he'd hustle against the
totters an raid scrap off the backa their drays. ohr days he'd scour
the firms at blackwall yard & masthouse terrace pier fer a job in
which he no longer had t put on a cockney accent, but could afford
t take out onea the laundry girls who shared their choclate with im
an laughed at his clothes on their way goin t work . . . *like repays
like*, he often liked t tell me, an when i came here eighteen months
ago—a decade older than he was then, an with a callin back home
t make the pied piper's spit valve seem permanently stopped with
motor oil—our rooms luked different, but the plot ran much the
same: under an assumed surname and wi digs on the bottom floor,
ad some times take his prayr card out an lean t wards the door.

london mixtape

I

say ye go fer a walk near clerkenwell green. say it's november, and the sertraline rattles yer bones like the shackles on jacob marley's wrists—*you may be an undigested bit of beef,* you think. *a blot of mustard*—though the night swings gently off the alexander mcqueen buildin, an the time fer thinkin yer happiness unreal has melted intae yer toffee nut latté.

2

the soup digs down between the polymers of the disposable carton
ye wanna save fer overnight oats. burrowed within the subatomic,
so that the non-scratch super-absorbent scourer ye use just won't
cut it fer the lingerin smella garlic. these are the days before ye can
afford bowls, an by then yer anger has pitched itself so far above
the fire alarm goin off across the street, that when ye finally fling yer
keys across the room an scream that ye wanna kill yerself, the fire
brigade arrives an you think that they're there for you.

3

the streets here lie thick as forest strata an dumber than god, though t night they luk well. in an alley behind yer flat, a man nods off with his trousers round his ankles. a security light flashes agin the brown brick tenement facin intae the courtyard, and as ye drift off t sleep, ye whisper to yer girlfriend that it reminds ye of *rear window*.

london poem

in which we bully home intae coherence. in which rooms distend
wi pizza boxes, HDMI cables, glassesa pinot grigio, an libraries
of unreturned library books. in which *measures of expatriation*
becomes a handbook for negotiatin the tube—*language is my home,*
alive other than in speech. in which articulation moves through the
ingredients culled from our shoppin list: garlic, choclate, regular
white bread . . . in which norishment is spread, mouth t mouth,
skin t skin, an our *salt rebuff* t england has less t do with speech, an
more the small republic sprawled across our mattress.

the depression

sprawled across the teak & brass rail bar,
suppose it's september 1932
and you haven't worked since broadway.

wouldn't *you* sit and just get drunk?
tell your folks you're meeting friends
in a drugstore on beachwood drive

then beeline up the trail to mount lee?
imagine the black fry of manure
& gardenias. all them crickets.

LA's bristling dark & yellow
like a bumblebee's fur.
downhill through hosiery & scrub

to HOLLYWOODLAND, and up the first
few rungs of a workman's ladder,
you see your face in a small ravine.

do you fall backwards or forwards
off the H, prefer it for its sigh—
in some quarters not pronounced at all—

or simply jump? one day vies
against the next, and for every kernel
of untruth you're just like a rosary bead.

your own ghost calls it through
and two policemen make the find: face down,
well-dressed, shoes & jacket in a parcel.

debt

two steamin hot cupsa green tea wi jasmine—
an it not yet bein lunch—am awoken again in
mid-conversation by a customer complainin
about the big six price hike. this mornin, the
job agency called an said that ad missed the
deadline for payroll by a day. i make seven
sixty an hour an won't get paid again until the
enda next month, so i nearly tell this bill payer
that, *yis bror, i hear ye*, but decide better of it
—preferrin instead to collect my frustrations
an pin them in *post-it* form t the sidea my
monitor—like prayrs at the sitea my own
wailin wall, or leaves on the bougha some self-
renewin weed.

the regulars

there we wor, us labour club regulars, sat hunkered around the scorched end of a woodbine gasper, waitin for d'arcy an discussin the horses. we said things like, *we're all baten dockets here son*, and *stand us one paddy an i'll get ye when am solvent*. because as paddy well knew, the luck of us men was perpetchally on its way, havin its progress hampered by critical luks from the omniscient wife, or bein decanted down storm drains by paras who blocked off roads and butchered dogs, by men who damaged heirlooms and battered childer. anyone could see these were hard times, and when d'arcy finally appeared, he was wearin a moth-eaten crombie an his face was hidden behind a reconditioned tea cosy. someone told us later that he'd had a six-shot revolver stuffed inside his pocket. others of us remembered that it was a finger pressed agin the inner linin of his coat. Nivertheless, once he waded out across the clubhouse floor, he was like a buckshot goose negotiatin water, and it soon became clear that he intended to have us robbed . . . the coffers of our takins in vital need of *redistribution*. the excitement in his hands made manifest by their shakin. so he pipes up, t no one in particular, *p-put yer fuckin hands up and open that there till*. to which paddy responded, cool as ye like, that if a single fuckin penny went missin it'd be added t his tab and doubled three times over. t which d'arcy relented and ordered a rum & black; his drink-blighted face still caught inside its cosy, his sloped malnourished shoulders still wrapped inside their crombie. this was in the seventies an though am really not sure how, there'd come a time much later when he was twice elected mayor.

cocktails

because we're in *bellini's* on merchants quay—still reelin from the
public display of affection near margaret sq—i order somethin
rough & warm, wi lotsa whiskey, which the barman introduces
as *old fashioned* an tops off with a twista lemon an floatin ball of
crushed, smooth ice.

you order a *dark & stormy*, which is described by the menu as bein:
fiery, refreshing, sweet, shaken & served long, an i can't help but think
that wiv each just ordered ourselves from the bar, as though our
tumblers wer lined wi the elixir of poolside narcissi, or an oubliette
driven through the highball lukin glass.

barcelona!

we said toger, an hour off the transfer
from dublin to gerona, gerona to . . .
barcelona! the *estació nord* quieter than
our unopened catalan phrase book,
midnight drapin her navy-dark trousers
over the closest spinnin hemisphere.
and so barcelona emerges like a half
remembered gerund, where over the
comin days we'll sleep soundlessly
with the drapes open, dodge past club
promoters hawkin strip & mojito bars,
eat paella on the steps of las ramblas
food market, then talk & make love
until our bloods have mutinied, and we
feel as though wiv lived this before &
might live it again, or else that someone
else has & would, and that we might
likely follow in their wake. over the
comin days we'll drink gin from bowls
the sizea shrunken heads, eat pistachio
nut ice cream, look out intae the
harbour at night & watch the distant
lights cast by mountain dwellins on the
water, as though mountains continued
underwater, all of barcelona sweepin
by us in the time it takes to run through
bob dylan's 115th dream.

sand mandala

not flesh as back t dust, but dust itself
made flesh by the myriad scrapinsa men,
the sand mandala took shape that mornin
in front ova crowd who'd stopped t watch
the monks at work—their bodies stooped
over a large clean slate, outlinin gods
wi T squares & rulers, french corves & compasses—
a thing i knew would take weeks t finish,
an longer again t forget the memory of.
so once it started, its progress seemed all
there was, an i checked daily t see the image grow—
the *kalachakra* in granules of crushed stone,
scraped from the *chak pur* for each dyed figure—
until the day when the monks removed it,
an took the sand in a silk-wrapped urn t the sea . . .
whereupon, you & i, my love, two particles shuk
from the residue of a dead picture, were dropped
by the wind intae our own fresh masterwork.

to the seven picassos missing from the art gallery of ontario

where wor ye?

i paid $11 to walk around in your absence for two hours an my hangover niver found bottom.

wat gives?

even hammershøi put in an appearance . . . albeit that his wife had torned away from him, an his attention was distracted by a seriesa blank etchins on the opposite wall.

your absence caused quite the stir, even if—after standin in fronta norval morrisseau's *man changing into thunderbird* for twenty minutes—my heart seeped intae the gallery's maplewood floors an accidentally dyed the vieira da silva downstairs.

all i could think about was my bror bein alone in this well-ordered & friendly city, an i nearly daubed yer stupid fuckin seventy-year career all over the walls;

popped my craniocervical junction like a jara bolognese an laid down my skull in placea your *death's head*, 1943.

the shift

only after comin outta the pool
      ontae clanrye avenue—
& haven't a fuckin baldy what way
      i need t balance myself
for the heat vent not t blow
      its chlorinated breath out
ontae the hay-dry grass beside us—
      when i start t notice these
broken bottles & roaches
      litterin the bank between
jack mackin & frank curran park;
      the word MUJAHIDEEN
sorta hangin there scrawled
      across onea the brook's
concrete bollards like a portent . . .
      so i says to her luh,
how the fuck am i sposed
      t follow through on this?
our whole arrangement's
      got less to do wi havin
our end away than havin it
      over with & thon corrugated
tin-walled bungalows beyond
      the carpark are only after
flattenin into a lane leadin
      out ontae cecil st.
purse, she says. *for fuck's sake.*
      stick yer fuckin tongue out.

INTERNMENT

clegs & fuckin

blue arsed flays

stun themselves fatly

agin the tobacco

stained porthole

above my door

out on derrybeg drive

a couple of kids

are draggin a roll

of chain link fence

off a concrete post

an up by main avenue

heaney's snug as a gun

is bein tapped out

in stones & bottles

against a paint covered

saracen soon

they'll be here

t smash

my ma's old bureau

to crack the sacred heart

wi their boot heels

to stick their rifle butts

through the sittin room

cabinet where i've kept

mi AOH sash pinned

to its backboard

like a moth

           balled weddin dress

                      for twenty five years

down there for dancin

           ye brit cunts

                      my heart exploded

two days ago

           durin grandstand

                      an all you'll find nai

is a stack of old papers

           a teacup brimmin

                      wi mould

a tartan quilted

           shoppin trolley

                      an my grey face

grinnin up from the shag

           t the bin lidded

                      chorus at st brigid's

ritual

a former paratrooper told the coroner's court how a colleague
recovered part of the skull of [a] man killed in the area . . . and
used it as an ashtray.

— the irish news, 2019

eventually it came to the point where we looked at witchcraft . . .
ireland was very superstitious and all we had to do was bring it
up to date.

— captain colin wallace, head of british army 'black operations'
in the north of ireland

ach, charlie! mind we usetae pull on our new rocks
and hunker down t chuckie ned's of a friday
with a gram wrapa coke down one of our socks?

mind that young fella was in a bad way—
martin sometin—and when he glimpsed thon blade
he lay down in the grass and passed away

before we cud ritualise our ambuscade?
wee prick nearly ruined the ceremony . . .
luckily, marianne had offset the nightshade

wi some potion she'd fixed with antimony,
and before ye knew it, he was on the altar—
ballin his lamps out t hell's cacophony.

mammy! this, and, *o jesus!* that. uncalled for
yappin as the athamé split his breastbone
and opened his chest like a demonic psalter.

the wounded knee incident

wi carragher pinwheelin around *the wounded knee*
on church st—*because the father says so, e-yayo*—
ida thought this ghost dance might curb the madness
now ripplin through him like a deafenin salvo.

forgive me, *até*, fer ave not bin entirely honest . . .
here—though knees are shucked like mountain oysters—
piss-stained tweeds stand in for feathers & calico.

each night, our enemies are backwashed intae a short,
an the blood of your/my ancestors is gurgled in retort.

hare—

or wor ye, instead, that mythic *giorria*
with his pelage tethered t the afterlife?
by the time ye'd arrived from edinburgh
and left knox, borke, mcdougal & yer wife,
rumours were already circulatin
that you were *the thing from tanner's close.*
maybe yer namesake lent t shape shiftin,
or yer fingers merely pinched the nose
a that other unsuspectin tenant—luck—
nivertheless, after the events at dumfries
people said ye'd vanished intae muck
with no accountin for yer whereabouts . . . at least,
that is, til ye crossed my path last saturday
when i knocked ye down on the M1 motorway.

clouds on a screen at a drive-in, n.j., 1960

so then allan & i went to the drive-in
in hoboken. mom looked after the kids.

and while we were filling up on gas
and getting candy along the way,

i bought a pack of flashbulbs & a pint
of *four roses* at about the same time

allan was tipping the attendant and telling
him go-nowhere stories about the war.

back then he'd talk about how family stores
like my dad's were repositories of memories

yet to be made. that each bar of soap sold,
suit made-to-fit, kitchen-set displayed

& dollar tendered was in anticipation
of a life as yet unburdened by collapse.

that photographs, too, fulfilled this need
to anthologize and make tangible the fleeting . . .

so when i tell you that the picture we watched
wasn't very interesting, that's because it wasn't.

some old thing by hitchcock about a man
who kills a woman and all the suspense that

that involves. hardly worth the celluloid.
the picture i'd make would focus on a crescent

of buicks fords & cadillacs crouched
around a hovering still life of the moon,

wire strung lanterns strung low over
a picket fence behind a silver screen,

the night sky burned black into the foreground
& allan asleep beside me dreaming, *diane.*

writing poetry at 5am

is sometin like barricadin yerself
inside the archives rooma the four courts
in 1922 an waitin to be shelled,
eatin milk softened day-olds, drinkin porter,
watchin the sun rise through a knifeways
crack in the sandbags & legal texts blockin
the windae, clutchin at rosary beads, prayin,
varnishin yer rifle wi sweat, knockin
yer exploded body on the names & dates
that whisper above dublin in an empty plume,
settlin as soot atop the barricades,
becomin soil, inchin out the tomb
as grass an bein evaporated to make rain,
drinkin a durty glassa water, startin again.

the great pyramids of carlingford lough

what dreams i have of you, khnum khufu,

                                  ferreted away

in your hidden sepulchre

                         like oil under a seam of shale.

tonight you line

                            the banks of the clanrye

as riverweed plots to drag you in its current . . .

                            our sleeper in the valley,

coma-dreaming your way

                    through one of the world's great wonders,

and content to bother no one

                     so long as you're undisturbed.

come join me on the flagstaff

                   and watch the world gloam over

this black horizon like a protostar!

                         like a nenuphar—

buoyed upon the *maat*

                    of this sleech-dark universe—

and mounted on the barque

                     that we use to cross the *duat*.

the liberator

WITH a coxcomb's taste for single malt scotch
& game, hessians on the deal planks,
beeswax in the candle sconce, jawbox
in the scullery, and press bed in the french flat . . .
with a gas lamp on the bar top, churchwarden
on the bar top, manteau on the coat stand,
greatcoat on the coat stand, one thin curtain
covering the ragged face of a beggarman,
and a wolfhound lying with his snout covered
in sawdust, the liberator came to us
in the springtime of the year of our lord
eighteen hundred & thirty nine, and folded up
that *cotton umbrella with legs attached*,
mr philpot curran, whose thunder he snatched.

prosthetics

i.m. ciaran carson

granted aul jim was a bit of a space cadet. an granted, yes, that
     at the end he became so demented
the cops picked him up at two in the mornin huddled freezin
     beneath a blackthorn bush . . . but for a while there
the neighbourhood had a *character*. someone who'd perch in his
     paint-covered kitchen chair overlukin the rezzy,
and invite ye up to his garage for a *miller*. who'd call ye over in yer
     christian brors uniform,
for all the world lukin like a man still in his prime. there was
     nothin sinister in this. jim was older
than the queen an'd sometimes refer to is wife as *the hitler*. in fact,
     durin the war he lost a leg
after one of his own squashed it with a tank. two weeks in a field
     hospital in el alamein before the leg was chopped
and he was sent back home to live a good-natured life showin lads
     like me the prosthetic which he'd tap
with a shillelagh . . . jim was my first protestant friend, though
     i niver managed to make it t the funeral.
what puts me in mind of him is a poem written by anor friend
     about a man *he* knew called horse boyle.
horse flew missions over dresden durin the war an had finished
     out his days makin a kinda prosthetic
of the caravan he lived in out beyond carrick. by *prosthetic*, of
     course, i mean an extension of himself—

which all homes are—and which in this case is described by my
     friend as bein: *encroached upon by baroque*
pyramids of empty baked bean tins, rusts & ochres. this, in torn,
     puts me in minda mi own phantom limb
and whether ad be expected t extol the virtues of *friends* or *family.*
     nonea them, after all, coheres t an idea
of *oneself as an extension*, an even if they did are somewat
     diminished by the suggestion that they are.
prosthetics require sometin to have bin lost in the forst place, an
     since my life has essentially bin one long
steady process of accumulation up t now, each loss found becomes
     sometin else entirely. which is anor waya
sayin that unexpected loss can lead t unexpected gain. which is
     anor waya sayin, *mo chara,*
that of the gains you've given me, i now give back t you in the
     form of an outstretched imitation of the original.

no live organism can continue
for long to exist sanely under the
conditions of absolute reality

which is t say that no one gave a fuck
about the haunted house on st patrick's
avenue until it began t disrupt our
lives. which is t say, that by insinuatin
themselves intae our hive of activity,
they forced our hand with amulets &
sticksa bornin sage. by then the ghosts'
demands fer civil rights had gone so
far beyond what cud reasonably be
considered, that the knockin on the
walls became an insistent petition in
morse . . . a variable five demands
which stalked the halls & broke the
plates, gave whispers out t cold spots,
and opened up the windaes when the
house had bin locked down.

zeuxis & parrhasius

and then there was zeuxis & parrhasius.
the first painter's smiling, brush outstretched, beside
a grapevine, but the grapevine's a painting

and a family of birds are at the window starved
as urchin nomads, coming to land,
to probe, to settle their black hunger.

zeuxis feels the hot breath, the shaking breast, the tucked
quick angst of his rival, and finding the birds fooled
by his simulation of natural life,

is moved to laughter. now he must hold his tongue—
like a canvas clamped in an easel—and wait for the time
when parrhasius draws the curtain back on his.

*

and since the whole thing's imagined anyhow,
imagine being zeuxis . . . which is he?
self confident, or arrogant at the time

parrhasius is revealing his painting?
is his brow leaking? does he still feel his knees?
or has the shut-eyed blank of what's behind

the curtain finished him? has the distance tightened?
alone and mirrored clear in his enemy's eyes,
i have deceived the birds, he begins.

a beginning he speaks too early,
for he has shocked himself, shocked the birds,
and as he touches the curtain, shocked to find it painted.

postscript

that we could walk hand in hand down a road that naither takes us
home, nor ends, nor makes us tired t continue . . . that the significance
of it, i mean t say, hits me freshly each time it dissipates—like
breath freed from a pried sarcophagus, or the slipped refrain of an
air caught in a bar or ona bus or in a bookshop behind the stacks of
YA & SF—is a possibility which leaves me both terrified & elated:
replacin face after face til ivryone's face is yours.

ACKNOWLEDGEMENTS

Some fragments and versions of these poems have appeared in the following publications and I am grateful to the editors for featuring them: Abridged, bath magg, Granta, The Irish Times, Irish Left Review, Magma, Morning Star, The Moth, New Statesman, New Welsh Review, Orbis, Poetry Ireland Review, The Poetry Review, Southword, The Stinging Fly, and The Tangerine.

I'd like to thank my mentor and friend Ciaran Carson, who passed away in 2019. Ciaran was not only one of Ireland's finest writers, but a raconteur and wit who was always insightful, generous with his time and quick with an anecdote. He will be sadly missed.

Special thanks are due to the Arts Council of Northern Ireland (and in particular, Damian Smyth), without whose generous ACES funding this collection would never have been conceived. Thanks also to the Seamus Heaney Centre at Queen's University Belfast and the Irish Writers Centre in Dublin, for providing the space and guidance needed to finish these poems.

Thanks to the Society of Authors, who gave *bandit country* an Eric Gregory Award.

Thanks to Danny Denton, Cal Doyle, Declan Meade and Sally Rooney at The Stinging Fly, for having the faith to publish such a generous selection of these poems. Their editorial advice was invaluable.

Thanks to Darran Anderson, Stephen Connolly, Ryan Coogan, Emily Cooper, Jill Crawford, Mickey Hanna, Dominic Leonard, Tim MacGabhann, Méabh MacMahon, D. A. Powell, E. M. Reapy, Stephen Sexton, and Michael Naghten Shanks for being good friends, reading early drafts of this book, and providing much-needed critical advice.

Thanks to my wonderful agent Niki Chang.

Thanks to my editor and friend Don Paterson and the entire team at Picador for making this book happen; particularly Salma Begum whose insight and exacting eye has been invaluable.

Thanks to my parents Conor and Geraldine, my brothers Seán, Joe and Eoghan, and all my extended family for keeping me sane. I also want to include my two granddas, Anthony and Tommy John, whose presence—despite not being around to see this book published—I have felt during the entire writing process.

Thanks to my faithful dog, Thelma AKA Mrs Douz AKA M'Deux.

Thanks to the Irish lit community. Thanks to my hometown of Newry. Thanks to Kendrick Lamar for writing *DAMN*, Fleet Foxes for writing *Crack-Up* and Miles Davis for writing *Kind of Blue*.

And thanks, as always, to my partner-in-crime, love of my life and sometime carer Aimée Walsh. This is for you.

GLOSSARY

AOH – Ancient Order of Hibernians, an Irish Catholic fraternal organisation set up in the nineteenth century in opposition to the Orange Order.

An Phoblacht – *The Republic*, an Irish Republican newspaper associated with Sinn Féin.

Baten docket – Usually used to express self-pity, e.g. *I'm a baten docket* (a betting slip that has no value, i.e. 'a beaten docket').

Bror/Brors – Brother/Brothers.

Clegs – Horseflies.

D'Arcy's – A recently revived popular Irish whiskey which originated in Newry.

Down there for dancin' – *Use your head.*

Haven't a baldy – *Haven't a clue.*

Hoor – Probably a derivation of the pejorative 'whore', normally used to refer to someone who solicits sex for money, though in Ireland a 'cute hoor' can also refer to someone (e.g. a politician) known for dodgy dealings.

Luh – Look.

Nai – Now.

Sidhe – Fairy, a derivation of 'Aos Sí' or The People of the Mounds.

Space cadet – Lunatic.

Spricks – Sticklebacks (fish).

Themara – Tomorrow.

Thon – Probably a derivation of 'that over yonder', used to specify something, e.g. *That*.

Tiocfaidh ár lá – *Our day will come* (phrase associated with Irish Republicanism).

Toger – Together.

NOTES

Epigraph: Douglas Dunn, 'Landscape With One Figure', *Terry Street*, Faber & Faber, 1969.

Yew: The name Newry comes from the Irish *Iúr Cinn Trá*, literally: 'The Yew Tree at the Head of the Strand'.

currents: Contains lines from Arthur Rimbaud (trans: Wallace Fowlie), 'Le Bâteau Ivre'.

one dry tear punctuating 'bliss': A response (of sorts) to Douglas Dunn's 'Re-Reading Katherine Mansfield's *Bliss and Other Stories*' (*Elegies*, Faber & Faber, 1981). The title and last two lines of the poem are lines taken directly from Dunn.

about suffering: (Loosely) structured after W. H. Auden's 'Musée des Beaux Arts' (*Another Time*, Faber & Faber, 1940).

ghost estates: After Anthony Haughey's *Settlement*, 2011.

xanadu: (Loosely) structured after Samuel Taylor Coleridge's 'Kubla Khan'.

london mixtape: Contains a line from Charles Dickens's *A Christmas Carol*.

london poem: Contains lines from Vahni Capildeo's poem 'Five Measures of Expatriation' (*Measures of Expatriation*, Carcanet, 2016).

The phrase 'salt rebuff' is taken from Philip Larkin's poem 'The Importance of Elsewhere' (*The Whitsun Weddings*, Faber & Faber, 1964).

ritual: Connla Young, 'British Soldiers Used Shot Catholic Man's Skull as Ashtray', The Irish News, 11.05.2019.

Henry McDonald, 'Satanic Panic: How British Agents Stoked Supernatural Fears in Troubles', The Guardian, 09.10.2014.

hare—: Serial killer and bodysnatcher William Hare was rumoured to have been born in Newry sometime between 1792 and 1804. He was arrested and charged with sixteen murders in December 1828, along with his accomplice William Burke, but escaped before he could face justice in January 1829.

clouds on a screen at a drive-in, n.j., 1960: After Diane Arbus's *Clouds on a Screen at a Drive-In, N.J.*, 1960, Printed: 1971, Photograph: gelatin silver print on paper, Image: 306 x 456 mm, Tate / National Galleries of Scotland.

the great pyramids of carlingford lough: After Seán Hillen's *The Great Pyramids of Carlingford Lough*, IRELANTIS, 1994.

the liberator: Daniel 'The Liberator' O'Connell (1775–1847) was famous for, among other things, championing the passage of Catholic Emancipation in 1829. The experience described here of a visit to Newry in 1839 is loosely based on his travel diaries.

prosthetics: Contains lines from Ciaran Carson's poem 'Dresden' (*The Irish for No*, Gallery Press, 1987).

no live organism can continue for long to exist sanely under the condi-tions of absolute reality: The title is taken from Shirley Jackson's *The Haunting of Hill House* (Viking, 1959).

zeuxis & parrhasius: Structured after Seamus Heaney's 'St Kevin and the Blackbird' (*The Spirit Level*, Faber & Faber, 1996).